Thank you so much for prayer, suppo[rt] friendship
I love you beyound.
Love LaToya M. Nelso[n]

WOMEN WITHOUT FEARS

Prepared Purpose

LA TOYA M NELSON

Women Without Fears "Prepared Purpose" Copyright © 2019 by La Toya Marie Nelson All rights reserved. No part of this book may be reproduced or transmitted in any form or by any means without written permission from the author.

www.womenwithoutfears.org
www.womenwithoutfears.com
www.womenwithoutfears.store

Print ISBN: 978-1-54397-082-1
eBook ISBN: 978-1-54397083-8

Scripture quotations marked (NLT) are taken from the Holy Bible, New Living Translation, copyright ©1996, 2004, 2015 by Tyndale House Foundation. Used by permission of Tyndale House Publishers, Inc., Carol Stream, Illinois 60188. All rights reserved.

Scripture quotations marked (NIV) are taken from the Holy Bible, New International Version®, NIV®. Copyright © 1973, 1978, 1984, 2011 by Biblica, Inc.™ Used by permission of Zondervan. All rights reserved worldwide. www.zondervan.com

Copyright © 2018 "Speak Into Your Own Life" by Margaret G. Green used by permission www.iamkingdomcreated.com "Tag Team by the Greens" 15 Minutes of Talk & Inspiration

Scripture quotations marked (GNT) are from the Good News Translation in Today's English Version- Second Edition Copyright © 1992 by American Bible Society. Used by Permission.

Scriptures marked KJV are taken from the KING JAMES VERSION (KJV): KING JAMES VERSION, public domain.

Scriptures marked AMP are taken from the AMPLIFIED BIBLE (AMP): Scripture taken from the AMPLIFIED® BIBLE, Copyright © 1954, 1958, 1962, 1964, 1965, 1987 by the Lockman Foundation Used by Permission. (www.Lockman.org)

DEDICATION

I dedicated this book to all the women in my circle of family and friends to break the cycle of generational curses by stepping out on faith and stepping over fears. Becoming who you are predestined to be. Walking in greatness and your prepared purpose in spite of what life obstacles have dealt you. Your failures and fears are designed to prepare you for purpose. I just love you all to pieces! I pray that you continue to be an example of God's love. I declare and decree blessings beyond overflow.

Table of Contents

Introduction ix
Reflection 1
    Day 1 2
    Day 2 3
    Day 3 4
Release 5
    Day 4 (Part I) 6
    Day 5 (Part II) 7
Worship 9
    Day 6 10
Prayer 11
    Day 7 12
Rejoice 13
    Day 8 14
Forgiveness 17
    Day 9 18
Prayer 19
    Day 10 20
    Day 11 21
    Day 12 22
Prepared Purpose 23
    Day 13 24
Authority 27
    Day 14 28
    Day 15 29
Faith, Endurance & Patience 31
    Day 16 32
    Day 17 33
    Day 18 34
    Day 19 36
Woman Without Fear 37
    Day 20 38
    Day 21 39
    Thought Reflections 45
    About the Author 59

INTRODUCTION

Lord as you prepare me for this 21 of consecration, I pray that you guide my thoughts and lead me to the right scriptures that will give a full understanding of this prepared purpose, allowing my thoughts, trials, endurance and faith be a blessing to others that are struggling on their journey toward purpose. Father I submit myself to you, help me to stay humble and honest toward all things. Lord you are my keeper, my strength, because of you I can and will do all things that you have ordained for my purpose. Thank you for everything I have and to come. Continue to protect my family as I obey your direction in prayer to pray down every stronghold and hindering spirit and release divine correction and direction. Bless every person that reads this 21 days of consecration. Lead them toward their prepared purpose. I pray that their mind be challenged to find salvation in you Lord and go forth. In Jesus name Amen

Reflection

Day 1

Going through pain is not an easy thing to bear. Some pain is caused from disappointment, grief, heartbreaks, brokenness, or even regrets. We often replay life events in our mind that reminds us of what has happen, while speaking aloud what could have been done differently. Yeah, I know because I do it too, it would it literally drive you insane if you let those negative thoughts take over your mind. **(Philippians 4:8 AMP**)*Finally, [a]believers, whatever is true, whatever is honorable and worthy of respect, whatever is right and confirmed by God's word, whatever is pure and wholesome, whatever is lovely and brings peace, whatever is admirable and of good repute; if there is any excellence, if there is anything worthy of praise, think continually on these things [center your mind on them, and implant them in your heart].*

Thought
- **Stop dragging your mind and focus on the goodness of God**

Woman Without Fear Daily Reading
Psalms 147:3
Psalms 34:18
1 Corinthians 14:33

Day 2

How did your first day go? Are you ready to make a decision on releasing your pain? Today you can decide to bury all things that has pulled you down, held you back, kept you from disheartenment, defraud you, or even made you feel powerless. Get your shovel and bury it deep in the ground and not in your mind. Affirm its finished in your life. (**Psalm 107:29 GNT**) *He calmed the raging storm, and the waves became quiet.*

Thought
- **Wake up and rebuke your storm**

Woman Without Fear Daily Reading
Psalm 27
Psalm 107:29

Focus
Psalm 27:11-14

Day 3

I know it's easier said than done is what you are thinking. Yes! I totally agree. The renewing of your mind will not just change in one hour, not even one day. We often try to psych ourselves to think those things that beset us didn't happen. (**2 Corinthians 10:4-5 KJV**) *"For the weapons of our warfare are not carnal, but mighty through God to the pulling down of strong holds;) Casting down imaginations, and every high thing that exalteth itself against the knowledge of God, and bringing into captivity every thought to the obedience of Christ"* In fact, your wrong because they did happen and its attached to your purpose. My purpose? Yes! Your purpose! Just stop and think for a moment.

Thought
- **Renew your mind with worship**
- **Release all negative thoughts**

Woman Without Fear Daily Reading
2 Corinthians 4:16
Ephesians 4:23

Release

Day 4 (Part I)

*Write down two things that you have overcame. How it doesn't affect you as much as it did the first time? Why?

___

(Romans 8:37 NLT) *No, despite all these things, overwhelming victory is ours through Christ, who loved us*

Thought
- **Nothing can separate me from the Love of God**
- **Thank Him for you being an overcomer**

Women Without Fears Daily Reading
Romans 8:35-39

Day 5 (Part II)

Follow up from Day 4

* Write your reaction. What caused your reaction? Think about everything …. Go Deep, Reflect and Release!!!

Reflect where you are right now in this very moment.

Thought
- Understand in every situation, you must be responsible we don't stand alone. You the individual responsibility is to be obedient to God. Then be faithful and loyal toward your reasonable service. He never leaves us or forsake us.
- Know that once we go off and do things on our own, we bear burdens of our sins. If your sins are continual, it effects everybody unless corrective action takes place

- **Thank Him for you being an overcomer**

Women Without Fears Daily Reading
Deuteronomy 20:8-9

Worship

Day 6

Question: Are you walking towards your purpose?

I challenge you to find a quiet place daily, channel your inner self and begin to worship God!

Thought
- **Worship in spirit and in truth**
- **Love on God (I adore, you are worthy, Your awesome etc.)**
- **Appreciate God (admiration)**
- **Go into a thankful zone**
- **Build or regain a deeper relationship with God**

Women Without Fears Daily Reading
John 4:24

Prayer

Day 7

Lord I pray right now for my sister who is reading this. Lord create in them a clean heart and renew within them a right spirit Father. I know that it is a challenge to let go of hurt and pain. But after yesterday God I know my sister will build a relationship with you and change her focus. Father, you have done it for me and I know you can restore all wounds, wounds that are dark and hidden Father, pain that we don't even talk about. I touch and agree with my sister that it be released and her healing starts now. Order her steps Lord. Give her courage with her head held up high in boldness, holding on to every promise that you have given her Father. Remind her daily that she is not alone, that you are with her always. Father today help her understand her purpose. You will begin to walk into it. Receive this prophetic prayer. Your healing is near my dear. Amen

Thought
- **Stay in the spirit**
- **Stay prayerful**

Woman Without Fear Daily Reading
Jeremiah 29:11

Rejoice

Day 8

Today is a new day!! Rejoice and be glad in it! You have more than enough reasons to be rejoicing. You are not dead sleeping in a grave and I know you have your right mind. Your healing slowing and what happened was supposed to have happened. Remember, ***Jeremiah 29:11*** reminds us of this. Sometimes I just had to chant it 30 times to understand God's Plan. Funny huh! I also used to chant "the Bible said be angry but sin not" ***Ephesians 4:26*** and how dare me to use God's word for my own personal way of thinking.

Sometimes we get so angry at the situations and things that make us mad or boil over. We forget to stop and pray. Remember God is in control and He knows what will happen before it happens. So if we don't seek God for all things……. BOOM a reaction occurs. It's was already in your thoughts and you gave your thoughts life.

Quiet? I know. I had to figure this thing out and go to God in prayer and ask for forgiveness so many times. Most of the time I knew better. Questions would disturb my mind with; How could I do this I'm saved? I have the Holy Ghost I'm saved. FLESH and EMOTIONS!!!!! I began to cry and beat myself up about my actions. Afterwards, I went to a quiet place, meditated on God and didn't move until I heard His voice saying "Hide me in your heart". ***Psalm 27:5*** KJV

I pondered for a while with tears flowing for about 30 minutes or more. I reached for my bible it opened right to this ***Jeremiah 17:9-10***. WOW!!! Still in tears. TALKING ABOUT A RIGHT NOW WORD!!!! Those thoughts were already in my heart because of the pain I had endured. God began to search my heart; the scripture was a reminder to stay focused in the mind so my thoughts don't penetrate in my heart.

Thought
- **Don't Be afraid to forgive**
- **That very second I knew forgiveness was required.**

Woman Without Fear Daily Reading

Psalm 26:2

2 Corinthians 13:5

Forgiveness

Day 9

Forgiveness can be very hard in some cases. However, forgiveness can be that very thing that is holding you back. I had to revisit yesterday's thoughts, emotions and actions. I found myself in a place of un-forgiveness and began to get weak in my worship. I was in a conflict worship. Running toward Jesus but feeling nothing. That moment I knew I wasn't true with my forgiveness because I wanted that person to feel exactly what I felt or even worse. Sad isn't it …Don't deny what you are feeling, release it and be free. *"A house divided cannot stand"* (**Matthew 12:22-28 KJV**) I had something inside that only the Spirit of God could drive out. Yes, LORD!!!

Take a moment a be truthful with yourself you have too. Admit it! Its ok we are working towards deliverance together. Forgiving a person doesn't happen overnight, it takes time. Most of the time we think we have to see the person that we need to forgive or them see us. I found out that's not true. The distance helps us in many ways. It allows you to refocus and gain strength if your sincere about your forgiveness. Pray with a sincere heart is a start. Never force someone to forgive you it will happen in its own time. You just do your part and not a quick fix…it will increase damage by not walking in truth.

Thought
- **How long did it take you to truly forgive someone?**

Women Without Fears Daily Reading
Psalm 130:4
Acts 10:43
Acts 26:18

Prayer

Day 10

Lord I thank you now for giving me a forgiving heart and a willing spirit to pray for those that have wronged me do to their selfishness, those that have been untruthful, those that have betrayed me. Father forgive me for not forgiving them. Teach me how to forgive those that despitefully use me, that have betrayed me, that harmed me, that lied on me and to me, those that haven't forgiven me. If I have done the same to anyone please Father bring it to my attention so I can make it right. Continue to create in me a clean heart and the renewing of a right spirit. I cast down every imaginable thought that holds un-forgiveness in my heart. Because with you all things are possible and that one thing that I desire is for true forgiveness to live in me. Amen

Thought

- **Let It Go, forgive yourself work on forgiving others.**
- **God forgave you first**

Day 11

It starts with you, forgive yourself and then work on forgiving others. Un-forgiveness holds us back and stops you from that very thing that leads you towards your purpose.

Yesterday, God allowed me to start off with this prayer and just mediate. Un-forgiveness is draining it can weigh your spirit down. It also affects your body, and soul. Our un-forgiveness often is towards someone that is close to us. Perhaps a best friend has shared your secret and you felt betrayed. A spouse has cheated and your heart was broken. Someone close has lied on you or to you and you felt angry. You've felt rejected or unaccepted by someone and it makes you feel alone.

It's important to trust in the Lord and do good in spite of and dwell in His faithfulness. God commands us to forgive and trust the process of His will for your life. God's love is faithful and pure not like man.

It's only because we put all our trust in man instead of God.

Thought
- **Are you ready to forgive?**
- **Will you trust God?**

Woman Without Fear Daily Reading
Micah 7:5-6
Proverbs 18:24

Day 12

Why are we still having a hard time on forgiveness? That's because we try to do it by ourselves. Get your hands out of God's business and allow Him to work. You could still be fragile at heart. Confused in your mind and having uncertain thoughts. My question to you is.

Are you mediating and focusing on hearing the voice of God? I know it's hard because the enemy wants to keep reminding you of your pain, those mistakes, disappointments, you think your unforgiven and haven't been forgave. Sister, I promise you if you keep your mind stayed on Jesus, his love, faithfulness, grace and mercy will bring you out of that place of doubt, shame, and excuses.

I dare you to go be free and stay free in Christ Jesus!!

Thought
- **Remember you are a new creation and old things have passed away**

Woman Without Fear Daily Reading
2 Corinthians 5:17-21

Prepared Purpose

Day 13

What a wonderful day of prepared purpose!! Prepared purpose...Yes... Purpose that was ordained just for you.

Stop and write down what you are thinking when you hear PREPARED PURPOSE. OH...I feel a prophetic word about to be spoken JESUS!!!!

_____
_____
_____
_____
_____
_____
_____
_____
_____
_____
_____
_____
_____
_____
_____

Did you know God knew what was going to happen even before it happened? Are you being prepared in your purpose? Well. Are You? I hope you caught it, if not read it until you do and let it sink in. God spoke this prophetic word to me.

Your pain brings forth your purpose. If you don't have pain your purpose is delayed. ***DEAL and BE HEALED!!!*** If it didn't come through pain it perhaps wasn't significant enough because I know that Pain + Purpose = Promise and brings out a PUSH. That's right my brokenness pushed me toward God whom which my Purpose is in. ***When I found my PURPOSE in God I began to live in PROMISE…after my promise was revealed I couldn't help but PUSH it out. Shout JESUS!!!***

Stop giving birth to things that's not attached to you. Once a woman becomes pregnant she is nurturing what's in (HER) womb. So if God is getting ready to release you for something, He nurtures (YOU) in the spirit and when its full term there goes that PUSH…STOP PUSHING BEFORE YOUR DUE DATE!!!

Thought

- **Hold fast to your promise and thoughts that God thinks for you.**
- **Continue to stand and believe in your purpose you are getting closer than you know it to it.**

Woman Without Fear Daily Reading
Jeremiah 29:10-14
Revelation 21:4

Authority

Day 14

Did you know that God want us to reassure our authority in Him? God's authority is unconditional and absolute. Woman without fears we are given certain authority to exercise. The authority as a mother, a praying wife, a leader, a business owner or a believer that ministers in Jesus' name. Remember there is no other authority other than that of God Himself. It's either ***derived*** or ***intrinsic*** authority. Do it so God's glory can be revealed. Live by example, while walking within your God given authority.

**derived-being, possessing, or marked by*

intrinsic- belonging to the essential or constitution of a thing https://www.merriam-webster.com/

Thought

- **Are you walking in authority?**
- **Reassure your authority and walk in it!**

Woman Without Fear Daily Reading
Romans 13:1
Psalm 29:10

Day 15

Women Without Fears Guide on how God's authority is ministered

- Patience - 2 Peter 3:15
- Leadership - 1Timothy 4:12
- Wives – 1 Peter 3:1, Ephesians 5:22
- Peace - Hebrews 13:20
- Kindness - Psalm 100:5
- Gentleness - 2 Corinthians 10:1
- Joy - John 17:13
- Forgiveness - Exodus 34:7
- Justice - Deuteronomy 10:18
- Wisdom - Romans 16:27
- Faithfulness - 1 Corinthians 10:13
- Truthfulness - Exodus 34:6, John 16:13
- Love - 1 John 4:8, Romans 5:8
- Goodness - Psalm 100:5
- Righteousness - Psalm 92:15
- Mercy - Psalm 86:15
- Compassion - Lamentations 3:22–23
- Holiness - Psalm 99:9, Romans 12:1-21
- Graciousness - Psalm 116:5

Faith, Endurance & Patience

Day 16

(Hebrews 11:1 KJV) Tells us "**Now Faith is the substance of things hoped for and the evidence of things not seen**" Jesus gives of faith to move. Even when we don't see the things that we have hoped for, it's still in reach by faith. Ask yourself what are you doing to walk into what your hoped for. Are you trusting God? What's your actions? Believe it! Do it! Then receive it! My grandfather always told me faith without works is dead. Activate your faith so that you can walk victorious in authority, which was already given to you. Stop laying down on negative faith. Your only worried about what could go wrong negative faith brings destruction, positive confession brings salvation. Stop wavering your faith, people will always distract to destroy by not agreeing with your faith. But guess what it's your faith. (laughing)

Just ask God to give you hope in the evidence of the things unseen. Whose report will you believe.

Thought
- **Activate your Change and commitment**
- **Limit your Time and Energy**
- **Focus on your Mind Body and Soul**
- **Don't be afraid to share your story, everybody wants to be inspired, but don't want to take action**

Women Without Fears Daily Reading
Hebrews 11
Roman 3:4
Isaiah 53:1

Day 17

Stop worrying about everything. Instead pray about everything, tell God your needs and don't forget to thank Him for His will being done. Even if it's not what you want to hear, still thank Him in advance. Remember you are a woman without fears and walking into your prepared purpose no matter what. You made the choice to trust God and I can assure you if you do this you will experience God's peace. Which is far more wonderful than the mankind's peace. Only the peace of God will guide your hearts quiet gives rest as you trust in Christ Jesus. (***Philippians 4:7 NIV***) Stop dragging your mind and focus on God's goodness. Stay in positive confessions and let the holy spirit create a solution.

Thought
- **Do something different to get something different. Remember that God could never get the glory out of your life if you quit.**

Woman Without Fear Daily Reading
Philippians 4:6-7
Psalm 27:14
1 Peter 5:5-7

Day 18

Today is your Faith Day…Speak It!! Today is my faith day…I will not lay down with negative faith. I will not speak against what God already promised. (deactivate negative faith) I will knock so Jesus can, I will continue to seek into I find. **(Matthew 7:7)**

Having faith is simply God showing you the things of your heart. If believe in those desires that are unseen. The father will truly grant you them. Your faith should be the size of a mustard seed, that's all it takes to believe what God said He will do.

Pray and ask God to give you hope in the evidence of the things unseen.

Did you know praising God is an act of faith and will help your faith grow? You can't have faith without taking constructive steps of obedience. Act on what God is saying. When you start to perceive who God really is, His faithfulness, love and power. Your faith and trust in Him will grow.

Thought

- **Can you remember one thing you asked God for and wasn't sure if you received it**
- **Think about…...Write it down**

_____
_____
_____
_____
_____
_____
_____
_____
_____
_____
_____

Woman Without Fear Daily Reading

Romans 1:17

Hebrew 13:15

Matthew 8:26, 9:29, 15:28, 17:20

Day 19

I can remember asking God for patience. My patience was not the best, I was the type of person that when things didn't go my way. I did something about and it wasn't praying. I either ran from the problem, started over because waiting was never an option in my book. It just appeared to be the right thing for to me but only what you do for God and in God will last.

The last situation that I was in really tested my patience. My back was up against the wall, very impatient. Like Gosh! However, this time around I prayed about it and didn't know at that time God was giving it to me. I was so humble with humility I couldn't do nothing but cry and begin to thank Him. I was driving my car and God spoke this very word "I'm hiding you" I started crying more I had to pull over. I called my Apostle Joe Green Sr., he was in the store and couldn't talk. Next, I reached out to his wife, my First Lady Edna Green and my sister in Christ whom is a Prophetess Margaret G. Green, she clicked in on the line. What I needed was for them to touch agree with me in the spirit on what God was speaking as I was praying it was confirmed again. By faith, patience was given to stand still because I was hidden in Christ. How do I know? Belief! I took myself out of it and God had full control.

Thought

- **Even if you can't see it yet, when the moment come it will be reveal.**
- **Wait in God in spite of timing and situations. What God has for you for you.**

Woman Without Fear Daily Reading
Proverbs 3:5-6
Ecclesiastes 3

Woman Without Fear

Day 20

Becoming a woman with fear wasn't easy. I had to go deep and channel my deep dark issues and create a release.

I too have endured physical pain, mental pain, heartbreaks, disappointments, and failures that caused fears. This was all a part of my purpose to understand what God was about to release.

The key to my peace, patience and endurance is knowing who I am and whose I am. Stop allowing people to dictate who you are. Never compromise right for wrong. Don't ever apologize for what God has called you to do. He wants to make you whole and give you all what He has for you even if that means letting go of somethings and being rebuilt for His name sake, while his glory is being revealed.

We as women be so afraid to walk in full purpose. I want to encourage you that it can be done. Stop being afraid!! One of my biggest fears was what would people thought of me if I served and loved God like I do. I was known as a hood chic and was proud of my street creditability, my anger was uncontrollable when extremely upset. What others didn't know was I was a woman after God's own heart, like David. However, I had a relationship with God. I don't just love Him I knew Him.

One-day God got my attention in a different way and I almost lost everything including myself. I'm not saying God didn't always have my attention, this time it was something about this particular outer body experience. It was like the willingness to suffer for something I truly believed in. I was willing to stay in the process of endurance and release all my fears for salvation and righteousness. I had to stop putting everybody needs before mine and refocus on the will of God pertaining my calling. ***(Matthew 20:16) "The last shall be first and the first shall be last: for many be called but few chosen.***

You have to be a willing vessel and put God above all things.

Day 21

So as you go about your journey and become a woman without fears. I want you to write a letter to yourself. List all of the things you are proud of and things you want to improve. List your accomplishments. List your dreams, goals and desires. Stay positive. You are a woman without fears.

Love Your Sister
La Toya Marie Nelson
Women Without Fears

AFFRIMATIONS

Woman Without Fear Daily Affirmation 1
I am happy
I am faithful
I am chosen by God
I am loved by God
I speak goodness to All
I fear no man but God

Woman Without Fear Daily Affirmation 2
I am a giver
I am a lover of God
I bless and not curse others
I am humble
My finances are overflowing

Woman Without Fear Daily Affirmation 3
I am wealthy in spirit
I am a speaker of truth
I am the head and not the tail
My steps are ordered
I am an asset and not a liability

Woman Without Fear Daily Affirmation 4
God is the head of my house
My house is blessed
My children are blessed and obedient
Jesus is the center of my marriage
No weapons formed against us shall prosper
I am kingdom created

AFFIRMATIONS

Woman Without Fear Daily Affirmation 5

My business is prosperous

I am a money magnet

I am seed sower

God is my shepherd and I shall not want

I represent the law of attraction

AFFIRMATIONS IN SCRIPTURE

Deuteronomy 6:13 NIV

Fear the Lord your God, serve him only and take your oaths in his name

Deuteronomy 7:19 NIV

You saw with your own eyes the great trials, the signs and wonders, the mighty hand and outstretched arm, with which the Lord your God brought you out. The Lord your God will do the same to all the peoples you now fear

Joshua 24:14 KJV

Now therefore fear the Lord, and serve him in sincerity and in truth: and put away the gods which your fathers served on the other side of the flood, and in Egypt; and serve ye the LORD

Samuel 12:24 NIV

But be sure to fear the LORD and serve him faithfully with all heart; consider what great things he done for you

2 Chronicles 19:9 NIV

He gave them these orders: You must serve faithfully and wholeheartedly in the fear of the Lord

Nehemiah 5:9 NLT

Then I pressed further, "What you are doing is not right! Should you not walk in the fear of our God in order to avoid being mocked by enemy nations?

Job 6:14 NIV

Anyone who withholds kindness from a friend for forsakes the fear of the Almighty.

Psalm 19:9 KJV

The fear of the Lord is clean, enduring forever; the judgement of the Lord are true and righteous altogether

Psalm 25:14 NIV

The Lord confides in those who fear him; he makes his covenant known to them

Psalm 34:7 KJV

The angel of the Lord encampeth round about them that fear him and delivereth them

Psalm 40:3 KJV

And he hath put a new song in my mouth, even praise unto our God; many shall see it, and fear, and shall trust in the Lord

Thought Reflections

Get into your word. They call you! Before God I thank you for choosing me + putting your hands of protection on me! You have shown me my help. Mt. Beulah was foundational for me. I can call on those people. It's not about being the loudest. (add to the prayer - ask God what (Before you enter the room + meet those people. You asking the Holy Spirit) Ask! (HS) what do you need said! Give me the words! + remove nervousness.

Thought Reflections

Thought Reflections

Thought Reflections

Thought Reflections

Thought Reflections

Thought Reflections

Thought Reflections

Thought Reflections

Thought Reflections

Thought Reflections

Thought Reflections

Thought Reflections

Thought Reflections

ABOUT THE AUTHOR

La Toya M. Nelson is a Wife, a Mother, an Author, an Entrepreneur and Woman of God, living without fear. In the pages of this book, she shares her story of God's redemption in her life and invites you to bask in the Glory of His process of breaking the stronghold of fear.

Are you a woman who has been afraid to seek out your purpose in HIM? If you are aware of your calling, have you found yourself afraid to walk it out? If so, I want to encourage you that it can be done! God wants you to release your fears.

2 Timothy 1:7 - For God hath not given us the spirit of fear, but of power and of love and of a sound mind.

One of my biggest fears was what people would think of me if I served and loved God like I do. I had been known as a 'hood chick' and was proud of my street credibility. My anger was uncontrollable when I got extremely upset. What those people didn't know, was *I am* a woman after God's own heart, like David. I had a relationship with God. I don't just love Him I know Him.

One day God got my attention in a different way and I almost lost everything, including myself. I'm not saying God didn't always have my attention but this time it was something about this particular outer body experience. I had an encounter with Him- a breaking. On this journey, I endured physical and mental pain, heartbreaks, disappointments, and failures that caused fear to take a hold in my life. This was all a part of my embracing my purpose- to understand what God was about to release.

The key to my re-establishing peace, patience and endurance has been the knowledge of **who I am** and **whose I am**. I hope that in my sharing, you find yourself encouraged to also find yourself in Him. I pray that you'll stop allowing people to dictate **who you are**. I touch and agree with you that you will never compromise right for wrong and that you won't ever apologize for what God has called you to do. HE is a restorer! HE wants to make you whole and give you all that HE has for you. I caution you, this process may include your letting go of some things and being rebuilt for His name sake. Come with me. Let His glory be revealed.